Inspiring Words
FROM THE PSALMS
FOR GRADUATES

_____

Presented to

_____

Presented by

_____

Date

Inspiring Words
FROM THE PSALMS
FOR GRADUATES

SPIRIT PRESS

Inspiring Words from the Psalms for Graduates
ISBN 1-40372-044-4

Published in 2006 by Spirit Press, an imprint of Dalmatian Press, LLC.
Copyright © 2006 Dalmatian Press, LLC. Franklin, Tennessee 37067.

Editor: Lila Empson
Writer: Phillip H. Barnhart
Cover and Text Design: Diane Whisner

06 07 08 09 WAI 10 9 8 7 6 5 4 3 2 1

14953

Because you are my help,

I sing in the shadow of your wings.

My soul clings to you;

your right hand upholds me.

Psalm 63:7–8 NIV

Contents

Introduction

The door you just entered leads to the rest of your life.

Beyond the door that leads to the rest of your life are opportunities with your name on them. Heaven will send you its gifts of options and openings each day. Prepare for them even before you know what they are. The greatest secret of success in life is to be ready when opportunity comes. Beyond the door that leads to the rest of your life are challenges that will test and measure you. If you call on God when challenges come, you will discover how vast and varied God's resources are and how available they are to you. When you look up to God for help, you can rise to any occasion.

You can find guidance for seizing opportunities and meeting challenges in the book of Psalms. As you go through the door that leads to the rest of your life, take the inspiring words from the Psalms with you.

You know me inside and out, you hold me together, you never fail to stand me tall in your presence so I can look you in the eye.

PSALM 41:12 MSG

At the Edge

The LORD will give strength to His people;
the LORD will bless His people with peace.

PSALM 29:11 NKJV

You are at the edge, not at the end. The resonance of the doors that are opening to promise and possibility drown out the sound of

any doors that are closing. Life's upside is on your side, lifting you to new achievements and strengthening you to new accomplishments. Hear and identify with the positive sentiment of Saint Paul, who said he could do all things through God who strengthened him. Your God is the God of possibilities. Your God is the God of power. Think of all the possibilities and power coming into your life right now as you stand at the edge of a vast panorama filled with the hope of a rich and full harvest.

As you stand looking at the possibility of harvest, view your future through the lens of anticipation. Have large expectations! When Wilbur and Orville Wright were working on their airplane, they said they couldn't wait to get up in the morning because they knew what was coming.

Stand on tiptoe, stretching toward what will be.
Awake each day to the thrill of what God brings.

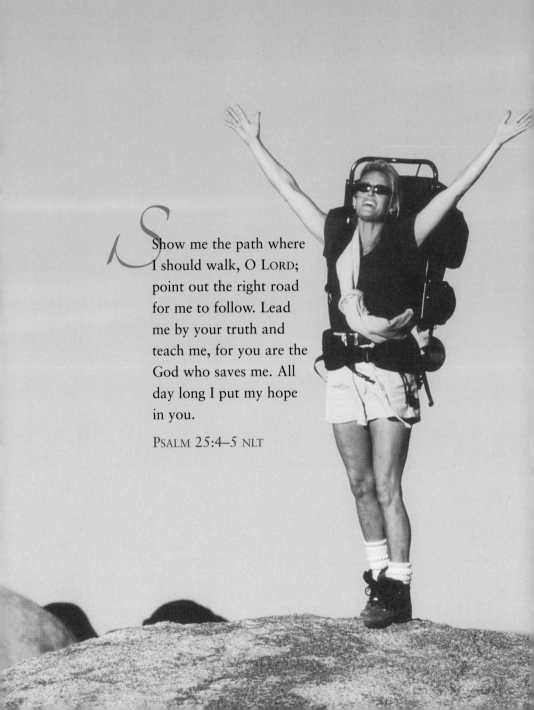

Show me the path where I should walk, O LORD; point out the right road for me to follow. Lead me by your truth and teach me, for you are the God who saves me. All day long I put my hope in you.

PSALM 25:4–5 NLT

One Step at a Time

Your love is ever before me,
and I walk continually in your truth.

PSALM 26:3 NIV

A house is built one brick at a time. Football games are won one play at a time. A business grows larger one customer at a time. Your

progress will be one step at a time. The tracks you leave will be put down stride after stride. Words make sentences, sentences make paragraphs, paragraphs make pages, and pages make books. And many books make libraries.

You don't have to see the whole staircase, you only need to see the first step and take it. Step after step, the staircase will appear, beckoning you to its top. If you stand still, you can't go forward, but if you step out, you'll move on. Step by step, stairs are climbed. Put one foot on one step, another foot on the next step, and after a while, you'll find yourself at the top of the staircase. You will have arrived because you began. You will have arrived because you continued.

All progress begins with an initial step.
The first movement is forward movement,
and the rest follows.

Every morning tell him,
"Thank you for your
kindness," and every
evening rejoice in all
his faithfulness.

PSALM 92:2 TLB

What God Wants

I delight to do your will, O my God;
your law is within my heart.

PSALM 40:8 NRSV

The best way is God's way. When you walk where God puts the markers, you stay on the path of God's will for you. That is always a large and blessed place. When you do what God wants you to do, you have harmony of soul and peace of mind. When you are connected to God's plan, you move forward resolutely and courageously. In harness with God's will, you keep step with divine purpose and eternal design. That makes all things better.

When Jesus taught his disciples how to pray, he told them to ask that the will of God be done on earth as it is accomplished in heaven. As you go forth from graduation, that same request is important and essential for you to make. Declare your intention to know God's will and to follow what you know. Fix your mind on discerning God's will and doing what you discern.

To know God's will is your greatest treasure.
To do God's will is your greatest pleasure.

The law of the LORD is perfect. It gives us new strength. The laws of the LORD can be trusted. They make childish people wise.

PSALM 19:7 NIrV

Make Somebody's Day

You are the one who put me together inside my mother's body, and I praise you because of the wonderful way you created me. Everything you do is marvelous! Of this I have no doubt.

PSALM 139:13–14 CEV

Each day, let people know how special they are. If you do this, you will give them joy. You will lift them up with a word of appreciation, get them going with a touch of assurance, and stimulate their effort with a note of affirmation. Those you affirm have their capacity increased, their ability unleashed, and their potential realized. That's what happens when you let other people know how extraordinary you think they are.

Speak words of affirmation to others ahead of schedule. Don't wait until they impress you with something they do. Let them know how much they mean to you by just being who they are. Talk about how much their presence brightens your day and lightens your load. Tell them how they make you feel good when they are around. Enumerate and evaluate their gifts to you. Remind them of what accrues to you because of who they are.

When you affirm others, you make the day brighter for them, more meaningful for you, and more satisfying for the world.

They give generously
to those in need. Their
good deeds will never
be forgotten. They
will have influence
and honor.

Psalm 112:9 nlt

A Great Combination

Hallelujah! Yes, let his people praise him as they stand in his Temple courts. Praise the Lord because he is so good; sing to his wonderful name.

PSALM 135:1–3 TLB

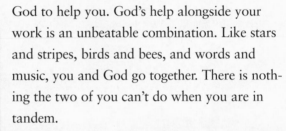

Whatever the task, work on it as hard as you can and ask God to help you. God's help alongside your work is an unbeatable combination. Like stars and stripes, birds and bees, and words and music, you and God go together. There is nothing the two of you can't do when you are in tandem.

Phylicia Rashad made theatrical history when she became the first African American actress to win a Tony for a leading role in a drama. She won the coveted award for her portrayal of a tough-minded matriarch in a revival of *A Raisin in the Sun*. When accepting the award in New York City, the actress stood behind the podium holding her trophy and said she had often wondered what it would take to reach such a milestone. "And now I know," she said. "It takes effort and grace, tremendous self-effort and amazing grace."

It takes self-effort and God's grace to accomplish your goals, achieve your objectives, and make your dreams come true.

I find rest in God;
only he gives me hope.
He is my rock and my
salvation. He is my
defender; I will not
be defeated.

PSALM 62:5–6 NCV

Ask for Help

Your people are wonderful, and they make me happy.

PSALM 16:3 CEV

As you go through the door to the rest of your life, ask people for help. There is much to gain and nothing to lose when you ask for assistance. You learn from those who know, from those who can.

A small boy was trying to lift a stone much too heavy for him. His dad walked by and asked his son if he was doing everything he could to move the stone. Thinking maybe he wasn't, the boy went into the house, got a crowbar, put it under the stone, and jumped up and down on it with all his might. The stone didn't budge. The boy's dad walked by again and repeated his question. "Are you doing everything you can to move that stone?" The boy replied, "Yes, Daddy, of course I am." The boy's dad disagreed: "No, you're not. You haven't asked me to help you."

You stand before a door that opens to the riches of information, knowledge, and wisdom. Ask for help.

You who live in the shelter of the Most High, who abide in the shadow of the Almighty, will say to the LORD, "My refuge and my fortress; my God, in whom I trust."

PSALM 91:1–2 NRSV

Up and Running

The LORD is a place of safety for those who have been beaten down. He keeps them safe in times of trouble.

PSALM 9:9 NIrV

Consider all difficulties and hardships that come your way as homework for life. Adversities you will inevitably experience need not be wasted. God does not intend for them to defeat you; he intends for them to grow and deepen you. They are designed to help you graduate to the next exciting stage of your development. Winter is preparation for spring.

Henry Roberts is the successful pastor of a large church in Florida. He is a man of great belief and deep faith. Henry Roberts is also a runner, and several years ago, while running along a city road, he was hit by an automobile and left to die. In a hospital for months, he talked to God and willed himself to return to his life and ministry. Henry Roberts is up and running again full-speed, every day and in every way. He would agree with Charles Spurgeon, who said he owed "more to the fire and the hammer than to anything else in my Lord's workshop."

Adversity introduces you to yourself and to the God who lives in you to help you grow through what you go through.

May the LORD answer
you in the day of
trouble; may the name
of the God of Jacob
defend you.

PSALM 20:1 NKJV

An Attitude Away

*May He grant you according to your
heart's desire, and fulfill all your purpose.*

PSALM 20:4 NKJV

All types of studies in various fields document the importance of attitude for success. What you want to effect or change depends a lot on how you feel about it. Of the five rules industrial psychologists consider for executive promotion, three of them have to do with attitude. One researcher went as far as to say that 93 percent of success is attitude, and 7 percent is knowledge and skill. Attitude, says another, is more important than facts, giftedness, or appearance.

When you face a task or meet a challenge, there are basically three things you can say to yourself. You can have a negative attitude and say "I don't want to do this." You can have a cautious attitude and say "I will wait and see." Or you can have an excited attitude and say "I can hardly wait!" Which attitude do you think brings success?

*What you accomplish and achieve depends
on your point of view. Tomorrow's success
comes from today's attitude.*

You will keep on guiding me all my life with your wisdom and counsel; and afterwards receive me into the glories of heaven!

PSALM 73:24 TLB

Be First

*Come and hear, all you who fear God, and I will
declare what He has done for my soul.*

PSALM 66:16 NKJV

From now on in your life, you will be doing much. You will be doing a job to make a living. You will be doing all kinds of things to make your family what you want it to be. You will be doing much, but it is important to first pay attention to who you are. Your *doing* comes forth from your *being* much more profoundly than your *being* comes forth from your *doing*.

Benson was the best employee Hector had ever had. He wasn't more qualified or better trained than the others, but his work had an unparalleled quality about it. It was more directed, and it was clearly inspired. It seemed everything Benson did came from inside himself. He knew who he was, and what he did on the job clearly indicated he understood that God had uniquely made him and greatly blessed him.

*Your actions flow from your being. What you do
comes from who you are. Be first, then do.*

You made them inferior only to yourself;
you crowned them with glory and honor.

PSALM 8:5 GNT

Blessings All Around

Bless the LORD, O my soul, and all that is within me, bless his holy name. Bless the LORD, O my soul, and do not forget all his benefits.

PSALM 103:1–2 NRSV

You will have a good life if you remember what a good life you have. To enjoy life fully, count your blessings. But can you count that high? Your blessings are too numerous to count, aren't they? Take pencil and paper and start writing them down. You'll run out of paper, and your pencil will wear down to a little nub. You'll find that you have much more than you thought you had. Blessings pour out upon you in an avalanche of bounty and benefit. As you sit at the table finishing one blessing, God will say, "Here, have another."

Happiness comes from gratitude. One person said, "I am too blessed to be stressed." Knowing how to live derives from knowing whom to thank. A seminarian visiting a monastery was eating fresh warm bread at the dinner table and asked one of the brothers, "Did we make this bread or was it given to us?" The monk smiled and answered, "Yes."

Count and recount your blessings. Know their vastness and their richness. Know their source.

You make the springs
pour water into ravines,
so streams gush down
from the mountains.

They provide water for
all the animals, and the
wild donkeys quench
their thirst.

PSALM 104:10–11 NLT

Believe You Can

Though an army besiege me, my heart will not fear; though
war break out against me, even then will I be confident.

PSALM 27:3 NIV

You have every reason to go through the door to the rest of your life with confidence. You are special because God made you. You are endowed because God equipped you. You have what it takes because God gave it to you. You can go through the door when you believe you can.

Your biggest challenge will not be to achieve but to believe you can achieve. That belief begins with knowing whose you are. You belong to God, and he has power to give you for each attempt and every endeavor. You can move forth confidently because you drink daily from God's deep reservoir. For every battle you fight, God gives you his full armor. Drinking from God's reservoir and equipped with God's armor, you have strength to endure and power to win. You are endowed with ability, designed for accomplishment, and engineered for success. You have what it takes.

You can have a ready supply of confidence
and act confidently in all things because
God is the source of your ability.

I am like an olive tree,
thriving in the house
of God. I trust in God's
unfailing love forever
and ever.

PSALM 52:8 NLT

God's Warning System

LORD, you have seen what is in my heart. You know all about me. You know when I sit down and when I get up. You know what I'm thinking even though you are far away.

PSALM 139:1–2 NIrV

Your conscience instructs opinions, forms decisions, and establishes positions. It helps you distinguish between what is wise and what is

foolish, what is good and what is bad, what is right and what is wrong. Your conscience is a bright and shining star that guides you to right actions and good behavior.

Be happy when your conscience hurts you. Be worried when it does not. A clear conscience is not always a good sign. A better sign is an inside voice that puts its hand on a proposed action and stops it from taking place. You will want to nurture your conscience for deep discernment and sensitize it to the most subtle of nuances. A small boy who, having been told by his dad that conscience is a small voice that talks to people when they have done wrong, went into his room and prayed, "O God, make the little voice loud!"

Your conscience is God's built-in warning system. It is your inner prophet. Listen to what it says.

*Y*our word is a lamp that gives light wherever I walk. Your laws are fair, and I have given my word to respect them all.

PSALM 119:105–106 CEV

Take Courage

*Wait for the LORD; be strong, and let your
heart take courage; wait for the LORD!*

PSALM 27:14 NRSV

If you want to do something important in your life, it will take courage. If you want to do something significant with your life, it will take courage. If you want to live your life meaningfully, it will take courage. Every life channel you surf will require courage. Courage makes everything stronger and better. Courage is a top item on every menu of action, a prime prerequisite for every achievement and accomplishment. Courage takes faith deeper, keeps love going, and turns the prediction of darkness into the reality of light. Courage is the drawer in which medals are found, the raceway on which records are broken.

In the midst of the Second World War, Winston Churchill spoke of courage when he said, "We need not fear that the tempest will overcome. Let it roar, let it rage, we will come through!"

*Courage stands in the middle of the ring, takes on all
opponents, and answers the bell for every round of
every fight. Courage makes everything more than it was.*

Be strong, be courageous, all you that hope in the LORD.

PSALM 31:24 GNT

All Around You

O LORD, how manifold are Your works!
In wisdom You have made them all.

PSALM 104:24 NKJV

You will have a good life if you look around and see what God has done. Acknowledging the bounty of God's creation is a great

source of positive thinking, a strong incentive for forward movement. Seeing the wonder and beauty of God in the intricacies and complexities of creation puts confidence in each step and provides strength for every action. It is difficult to look at a penguin and not feel good. It is hard to think of the wonderful seas and oceans God has splashed all over the world and not be lifted up.

When you have reverence for what God makes, your soul is furnished with positive thoughts and good feelings. You face a horizon of hope and promise. You walk toward that horizon on the high side of life, buoyed with anticipation and praise. You see creation as a vivid scene wherein God carries out his purpose and plan for you.

God's signature is written everywhere on the
garments of nature. Look around you, all
around you, and there is God.

You, O Lord, have
made me glad by what
You have done, I will
sing for joy at the works
of Your hands.

PSALM 92:4 NASB

Day by Day

Give praise to the Lord. Give praise to God our Savior. He carries our heavy loads day after day.

PSALM 68:19 NIrV

George Burns, the comedian, said he was good at "now." You will have a good life if you are good at now, alive and well in the present moment, open to the opportunities and possibilities right in front of you. There is a great deal of freedom when you live in the present tense. You are not encumbered by what has been or what will be. You are not locked in history or trapped in a vision of the future. You are free to act fully in the present and to find God in the moment.

God wakes you each morning and puts a day before you filled with promise and potential. Accept each minute of each day as a gift to unwrap, admire, and utilize. Each day God gives you is a miracle of life and living. Hold the miracle of every twenty-four hours tightly in your heart of appreciation and thankfulness. Your life is wonderful, day by day.

You are free to explore the promise of the day you have, to lift up its potential and weigh its prospects in the light of what is.

The LORD shows his true love
every day. At night I have a song,
and I pray to my living God.

PSALM 42:8 NCV

Decisions Change Everything

*Who are they that fear the LORD? He will teach
them the way that they should choose.*

PSALM 25:12 NRSV

As you go through the door that leads to the rest of your life, here is an important truth to take with you. Wishes change nothing, but decisions change everything. Successful people are ordinary people who made good decisions. They took Shakespeare's tide at the flood that led to fortune. They walked down Robert Frost's less traveled road that made all the difference. You will succeed if you choose well from among the branches of possibility on the tree of prospects. You will succeed if you raise your eyes confidently to the hills of options and decide wisely.

Indecision is the thief of opportunity. To not decide is to let openings close and watch chances vanish. You will not drift into achievement. On the other hand, good decisions clear the path on which you walk and put signposts of direction along the road. Good decisions know the way to success.

*Good decisions give you a plan and put you in
charge of circumstances. They provide direction,
create resources, and bring power for the task ahead.*

*H*ow sweet are Your words to my taste, sweeter than honey to my mouth!

PSALM 119:103 NKJV

Downs and Ups

You are my hiding place; you protect me from
trouble. You surround me with songs of victory.

PSALM 32:7 NLT

As you move on in your life, not everything will go your way all the time. Life is a series of ups and downs, and you can't change that.

Sometimes you will expect a rainbow and get only rain. When the actual experience falls short of what was expected, you will be disappointed. Every twenty-four hours the world turns on someone who was sitting on top of it.

On the job, in the family, and around the neighborhood you will have setbacks, but after every setback God promises the possibility of a comeback, even a comeback that puts you ahead of your previous pace. However hard you fall or how far you land from where you want to be, you can get up and start over again, more determined than ever because God is with you.

Knowing the power of God's helping hand, you can
get up and press on with the confidence of David
against Goliath. You can have the biggest
comeback since Lazarus.

He lifted me out of the
ditch, pulled me from
deep mud. He stood me
up on a solid rock to
make sure I wouldn't slip.

Psalm 40:2 MSG

Get All Excited

O sing to the LORD a new song, for He has done wonderful things,
His right hand and His holy arm have gained the victory for Him.

PSALM 98:1 NASB

Right now you are probably so excited you can hardly stand it. A life full of promise and possibility stands in front of you. Open waters of anticipation wash in upon the shore of your life, inviting you to adventure and accomplishment. The door to a bright and rewarding future has turned on its hinges and is wide open, waiting for you to enter. The road to triumph and success is at your feet. It is an exciting time for you.

Stay excited. When you are an excited person, you have an exciting life. When you get excited about your work, you have an exciting career. When you get excited about the people in your life, you have exciting relationships. When you get excited about how much God loves you, life is lived on the edge of expectation. When you get excited about the day before you, that day becomes an inspiring and stimulating experience.

Excitement sees opportunities and makes the
most of them. Whatever you do, add excitement
to it, and you will be successful.

*I'*m ready, God, so ready,
ready from head to toe.
Ready to sing, ready to
raise a God-song:
"Wake, soul! Wake, lute!
Wake up, you
sleepyhead sun!"

PSALM 108:1–2 MSG

Expect Great Things

In the morning, O LORD, You will hear my voice; in the morning I will order my prayer to You and eagerly watch.

PSALM 5:3 NASB

As you look to your future, expect great things to happen. Set lofty standards, and then work and live and pray your way up to

them. Put your ladder against a tall wall and begin climbing. When you reach the top of the ladder, pull out an extension and keep going. When you scale that wall, move your ladder to another one. Think big about what you can do with your life.

In a painting of the blind man at Jericho by the French master Nicolas Poussin, there is an interesting detail that usually goes unnoticed. In one corner of the canvas, there is painted a discarded cane lying on the steps of a house. The blind man sat on those steps with his cane in hand, but when he heard Jesus was passing by, he left his cane on the steps and went into the house fully expecting to see.

High achievement takes place in the context of high expectation. Expectations of success breed success.

LORD, I wait for you to help me. LORD my God, I know you will answer.

PSALM 38:15 NIrV

Stay at It

All the paths of the LORD are steadfast love and faithfulness,
for those who keep his covenant and his decrees.

PSALM 25:10 NRSV

As you go through the door to the rest of your life, set goals and stay at them. Be faithful to your objectives. Create dreams in your

mind and follow them with your heart. You can do anything if you stick to it long enough. Memorize Winston Churchill's six words for success: "Never, never, never, never, give up."

Wilma Rudolph was a tiny, premature baby who caught pneumonia, then scarlet fever, and finally polio. The polio left one leg badly crippled, with her foot twisted inward. But Wilma Rudolph did not give up. When she was eleven, she took off her leg braces and learned to walk without them. She progressed to running and, when she was sixteen, won a bronze medal in a relay race in the Melbourne Olympics. Four years later, in the Rome Olympics, she became the first woman in history to win three gold medals in track and field.

You conquer by continuing. Never fold up;
always hold up. When you want to give in, go on.

*You are my inheritance,
O Lord. I promised to
hold on to your words.*

PSALM 119:57 GOD'S WORD

Manage Your Money

Trust in the LORD, and do good;
so you will live in the land, and enjoy security.

PSALM 37:3 NRSV

As you go through the door to the rest of your life, you will have money for which you are responsible. Receive it as a gift, honor it as

a resource, and manage it well. Thank God for income, don't take it for granted, and use your money wisely. Your money is far more a responsibility than it is a possession. Your right relationship to money is to put it to right uses.

You can't take your money with you when you die, but you can send it on ahead in deeds of compassion and service. Money talks, and you can help it speak up on behalf of what is good and godly. Money talks, and the way you handle it says a great deal about you. It is an index of your priorities, an indicator of your value system. What you do with your money tells people who you are and what you stand for.

Money is God's gift to you. What you spend it on
is your gift to others, and your thanks to God.

*Y*ou will keep on guiding me all my life with your wisdom and counsel; and afterwards receive me into the glories of heaven!

PSALM 73:24 TLB

Take Care of Your Body

*The LORD will guard your going out and your
coming in from this time forth and forever.*

PSALM 121:8 NASB

One of God's gifts to you is your body. God wants you to respect and honor the gift by taking care of your body. If you don't take care of your body, where are you going to live? What will get you from place to place and enable you to function meaningfully and significantly?

Cherish your health. If it is good, preserve it. If it is not good, improve it. If it is beyond what you can preserve or improve, get help. Move intentionally and consistently toward good health. Health professionals say that more then half of the illnesses in this country are preventable. Most of the prevention begins in the mind and heart. View your health not so much as the absence of sickness, but as the presence of a rich and full quality of life made possible by God's gift to you.

Your body is wonderful. Make sure it gets the best of everything. You don't put cheap gas in a Rolls-Royce!

The righteous flourish like
the palm tree, and grow
like a cedar in Lebanon.

PSALM 92:12 NRSV

A Success Story

One day spent in your Temple is better than a thousand anywhere else; I would rather stand at the gate of the house of my God than live in the homes of the wicked.

PSALM 84:10 GNT

At graduation time there is much talk of success. It seems to be on everyone's mind. Formulas for success are constructed, recommended, and communicated. Goals are envisioned and objectives projected.

But success requires more than formulas, goals, and objectives. It requires a suitable method of evaluation. Jesus hanging on a cross makes him a loser to many, but at the moment of his death he cried out triumphantly that he had successfully completed what God sent him to do. Think about the life ahead of you and define for yourself what will make you successful. Ten years from now, will you have done what God wants you to do? Golda Meir, prime minister of Israel, said she was "never affected by the question of the success of an undertaking. If I felt it was the right thing to do, I was for it regardless of the possible outcome."

Success is the progressive realization of a worthy ideal. It is doing good work well. It is fulfilling God's will for your life.

Unless the Lord builds a house, the builders' work is useless. Unless the Lord protects a city, sentries do no good.

PSALM 127:1 TLB

God Wants to Bless

We praise you, Lord God! You treat us with
kindness day after day, and you rescue us.

PSALM 68:19 CEV

An insightful story tells of a rabbi who stopped a member of his congregation on the street and said, "Every time I see you, you are in a hurry. You're always running somewhere. Tell me, why do you do this?" The man thought the question unusual but gave what he perceived was a sensible answer. "I'm trying to make a good living. I'm running after success and prosperity." The rabbi complimented the man on his answer, but then posed another question. "What if all the things you assume are out ahead of you aren't really there at all and you run after them in vain? What if the rewards you seek are behind you? What if God has all sorts of wonderful gifts for you, but you are never home so he can give them to you?"

God is looking for you so he can bless you with
many gifts. Sit still, open your hands, and let God
fill them with the benefits of his bounty.

God's words are pure words, pure silver words refined seven times in the fires of his word-kiln.

PSALM 12:6 MSG

Watch What You Say

*Those who are planted in the house of the LORD shall
flourish in the courts of our God. They shall still bear fruit
in old age; they shall be fresh and flourishing.*

PSALM 92:13–14 NKJV

Your words are the windows to your heart. They declare what
you think and how you feel about what you think. Choose your
words carefully. They tell people who you
are and what you are about. Words repre-
sent you. Make sure they do a good job of
it. Use words in such a way that they tell
the truth about you.

Use words to say something important,
not just to rearrange the wind. The reason
Lincoln's 278-word address at Gettysburg is
remembered and Edward Everett's two-hour-long Gettysburg oration
is long forgotten is that Lincoln spoke a message while Everett said
some words. Speak your words into a message that says something
of value. Let them come from your mouth as ambassadors of princi-
ples and ideals. Whatever the length of your words, let their depth be
clear and obvious.

*The average educated person who speaks
English knows about twelve thousand words.
Use the ones you know well. Use them for
good. Ask God to bless each one.*

I meditate on your precepts and consider your ways. I delight in your decrees; I will not neglect your word.

PSALM 119:15–16 NIV

Make Beautiful Music

*I will incline my ear to a proverb; I will solve my
riddle to the music of the harp.*

PSALM 49:4 NRSV

It is true that you sing because you are happy, but it may be truer that you are happy because you sing. The first job God called David of the Bible to do was to make music. He

was to play sweet and soothing music to Saul so that the king's troubled soul might find harmony and order. In your life, music has the power to give order to confusion and bring harmony out of dissonance. It has the ability to take the disconnected notes of scattered experiences and line them up on the scale of plan and purpose. Music can find you lonely and connect you to a community of joy and celebration. It gives voice to the deepest of your feelings, substance to the undeveloped embryo of your ideals, and direction to the most hesitant of your desires.

*Music understands what you feel, think, and
wish for. It knows its way all the way to the
core of your heart and soul.*

I will thank the LORD because he is just; I will sing praise to the name of the LORD Most High.

PSALM 7:17 NLT

It's About Time

*You will arise and have compassion on Zion; for it is time
to be gracious to her, for the appointed time has come.*

PSALM 102:13 NASB

Each day you have time on your hands. What do you do with it?
Do you assign it to the unnecessary and the trivial, or do you give it
to the significant and the important? Do you let
it come and go as it pleases, or do you take
charge of the time you have and use it to glorify
God in the world where you live? Do you try to
get through the hours and days in front of you
in order to get to better ones, or do you see the
here and now as the precious bequest it is? Do
you reverence it as a gift from God? Is your life
like an airport, where you waste time waiting
so you can save time flying? Or is it like a bas-
ket of ripened fruit that you must eat right away for the greatest
enjoyment?

*Time is God's chronological gift to you.
It is your currency. Spend it well.*

The day is yours, and yours also the night; you established the sun and moon. It was you who set all the boundaries of the earth; you made both summer and winter.

PSALM 74:16–17 NIV

Laugh a Lot

Our mouth was filled with laughter, and our tongue with singing. Then they said among the nations, "The LORD has done great things for them."

PSALM 126:2 NKJV

In all aspects of your life, laughter serves you well. It opens doors closed by disappointment and clears roads trashed by failure. The

old folk saying that laughter is "God's hand on the shoulder of a troubled world" is true. Laughter gives perspective as nothing else can. It enables you to laugh with others and at yourself. Abraham Lincoln said laughter is "the joyous universal evergreen of life."

Laughter is like a pebble you sail across a pond that spreads its ripples over the water. Someone quipped the truth in this bit of doggerel: "I may be brash and I may be bold, but as long as I am laughing I won't be old." It is true that scientists have studied the effect of laughter on people and found that it has a profoundly positive effect on every organ in the human body.

Laughter is an endowment straight from heaven. It is a most precious gift and blessing that comes to you on earth.

You have made known to me the path of life; you will fill me with joy in your presence, with eternal pleasures at your right hand.

PSALM 16:11 NIV

Determine to Do It

The LORD God is a sun and shield; the LORD bestows
favor and honor; no good thing does he withhold from
those whose walk is blameless.

PSALM 84:11 NIV

As you pursue your goals, be a plugger who is willing to pay the price. See where you want to be, and determine to get there. When

Sir Edmund Hillary climbed Mount Everest, something no one else had done, he was asked why he succeeded when others failed. He said it was because he took one more step. Take one more step on the road to your objectives, and you will get there. Determine to keep going, and you will find or make a way.

During the excruciating sequence of political and military struggles from late autumn 1862 to early summer 1863, Abraham Lincoln's resolve concerning setting the slaves free strengthened rather than weakened. He told a friend, "I may be a slow walker, but I never walk back."

Diamonds are but pieces of coal that stuck to
their jobs. Stick to yours. God will honor
your resolve and determination.

Mercy and truth have met together; righteousness and peace have kissed. Truth shall spring out of the earth, and righteousness shall look down from heaven.

PSALM 85:10–11 NKJV

Read for Life

*Their delight is in the law of the LORD, and
on his law they meditate day and night.*

PSALM 1:2 NRSV

If you are a reader, you will live life down to its core and up to its pinnacle. Readers may not live longer, but they live better because they have tasted of wisdom and learned of power. Harry Truman told friends he was never bored as a child because his boyhood home was full of books. He had read the Bible through twice by the time he was twelve, and he later read all of the new set of Shakespeare that his parents had bought. Before he graduated from high school, he'd read nearly every book in the local library. Reading was his transport to the world.

The main library at Indiana University sinks more than an inch every year because, when it was built, engineers failed to take into account the weight of all the books that would occupy the building. Reading adds weight to your life. It makes you bigger and better.

*Erasmus said when he had a little money he
bought books. If there was anything left over,
he bought food and clothing.*

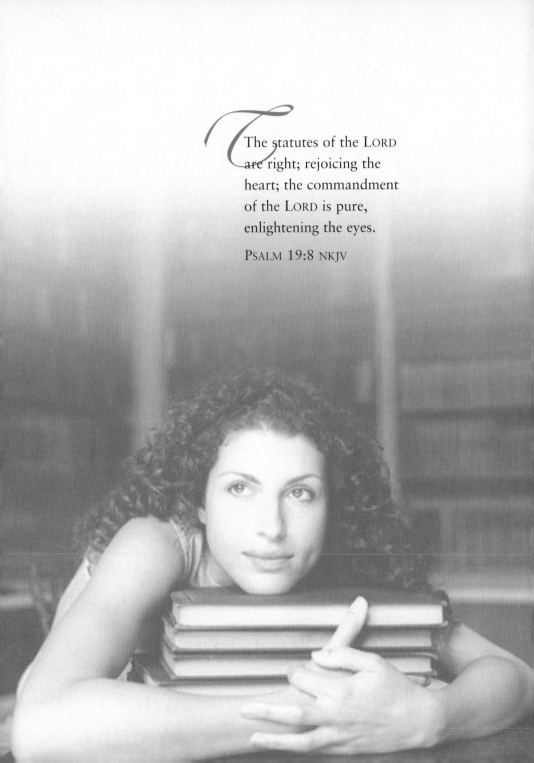

The statutes of the LORD
are right; rejoicing the
heart; the commandment
of the LORD is pure,
enlightening the eyes.

PSALM 19:8 NKJV

Be a Giver

He satisfies the thirsty, and the hungry he fills with good things.

PSALM 107:9 NRSV

You will be a better liver if you are a good giver. When you give your time, you enrich every minute. When you give your money, you know lives are changed and know you had something to do

with it. Give your talent, and watch projects flourish and causes prosper. Give yourself and know God's sure embrace of warm acceptance. You will make a living from what you get, but you will make a life from what you give.

Oseola McCarty washed clothes for more than fifty years in Hattiesburg, Mississippi. During that time, she saved $150,000, which she donated to the University of Southern Mississippi. Upon learning of her donation, President Clinton invited her to Washington and gave her the Presidential Citizens Medal. In that moment she knew the joy that always comes to those who are generous.

It is not what you gain but what you give that measures the worth of your life. What you give away you always have.

*H*appy are those who are
concerned for the poor;
the LORD will help them
when they are in trouble.

PSALM 41:1 GNT

Don't Worry About It

When anxiety was great within me, your
consolation brought joy to my soul.

PSALM 94:19 NIV

Worry is sometimes advance interest you pay on a debt that never comes due. A lot of what you worry about doesn't happen. Some of

it probably couldn't. When you worry disproportionately, you cast large and dark shadows on small things. Worry is too often your imagination run wild.

Don't worry; be positive. Hang on to the good things in your life and shake off the bad things. See your world as a place blessed by the gifts and graces of God. Be always jumping to positive conclusions about who you

are, what you have, and where you are going. On the occasion of his seventy-fifth birthday, General Douglas MacArthur wrote, "In the central place of every heart there is a recording chamber. So long as it receives messages of beauty, hope, cheer, and courage, you will be young."

Look for the best, seek the greatest, and
search for the beauty of the good. Think
positively and positively think.

Our soul waits for the
LORD; he is our help and
shield. Our heart is glad
in him, because we trust
in his holy name. Let
your steadfast love,
O LORD, be upon us,
even as we hope in you.

PSALM 33:20–22 NRSV

Be a Student

Comfort me with your love, as you promised me, your servant.
Have mercy on me so that I may live. I love your teachings.

PSALM 119:76–77 NCV

After graduation, be a student. Don't stop learning. Search and research. Read and heed what you read. Study to show yourself knowledgeable about many things. Be curious about what makes something work, what makes somebody think, what makes somewhere the place it is. Increase your vocabulary, expand your repertoire, push the envelope of what you know so far. The great basketball coach John Wooden said, "It's what you learn after you know it all that counts." Look, listen, pay attention. There is so much to learn. Use the mind God gives you to explore the world God gives you.

Live to learn, and you will learn to live fully and significantly. Life will be richer and deeper. People will be more interesting. Ordinary locations will take on unexpected meaning. God's everyday gifts will become obvious and exciting. Learning is the best of all wealth, the most genuine of all riches.

Keep learning. Don't ever quit wanting to know
what you don't know. Yearn to learn.

A white-tailed deer drinks from the creek;
I want to drink God, deep draughts of God.

PSALM 42:1 MSG

Use Your Imagination

Powerful is your arm! Strong is your hand! Your right hand is lifted high in glorious strength.

PSALM 89:13 NLT

Your imagination is God's gift to you. It is the place where your dreams and hopes begin. It is where you first see who you can be, where you can go, what you can accomplish. Imagine it, and believe it. Imagine it, and achieve it. Imagination is more important than knowledge. Knowledge is limited, but imagination goes everywhere. Imagination stretches far and wide but never breaks.

Imagination is a passport into your future. Imagine what you can be doing five years from now. Envision what your résumé will look like ten years from now. Think about whom you will know and where you will be twenty years from now. People tell you not to cross a bridge until you come to it, but think of all that has been accomplished by those who, in their imaginations, crossed bridges far ahead of the crowd.

Imagination is the first step of faith. It gets you going toward what can be. It propels you into what will be.

He determines the number
of the stars; he gives to all
of them their names. Great
is our Lord, and abundant
in power; his understanding
is beyond measure.

Psalm 147:4–5 nrsv

More Than You Think

LORD, who may enter your Temple? Who may worship on Zion, your sacred hill? Those who obey God in everything and always do what is right, whose words are true and sincere.

PSALM 15:1–2 GNT

You have more influence than you think you have. Drop your pebble in the water, and watch its ripples reach out far and wide. Who you are when you are with others affects their outlook on life. What you do when you are challenged teaches lessons of courage and fortitude. Your ideas are valuable; your commitments are important; your opinions matter. Your life impacts the lives of others.

When Phillips Brooks was at the peak of his influence as a pastor in Boston, a local newspaper said, "The day opened cloudy and cheerless, but about noon Phillips Brooks came downtown and everything brightened up." Did you ever think about the rest of the Good Samaritan story Jesus told? What effect did the Samaritan's good deed have on the one he helped? Did he remember that act and shape his life by it? Did he treat others as he had been treated? Was he influenced to be good, honest, and kind?

How you live your life is important to other people. They learn from you, and you inspire them.

*L*et the words of
my mouth and the
meditation of my heart
be acceptable in Your
sight, O LORD, my rock
and my Redeemer.

PSALM 19:14 NASB

Do It Well

Awake, my glory! Awake, lute and harp!
I will awaken the dawn.

PSALM 57:8 NKJV

Whatever you do in your life, do it well. The secret to joy in life is found in one word, and that word is *excellence*. There is no substitute for excellence, not even success. Make up your mind from the

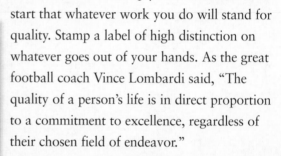

start that whatever work you do will stand for quality. Stamp a label of high distinction on whatever goes out of your hands. As the great football coach Vince Lombardi said, "The quality of a person's life is in direct proportion to a commitment to excellence, regardless of their chosen field of endeavor."

As you go forth from graduation into a career, give your very best to your work. Don't settle for average, because that means you're just as close to the bottom as you are to the top. You may not always have the best of everything, but you can always make the most of everything.

Give the world the best you have, and the best
will come back to you. It knows the way.

He counts the stars and names each one. Our Lord is great and very powerful. There is no limit to what he knows.

PSALM 147:4–5 NCV

Take Your Time

If I say, "Surely the darkness will overwhelm me, and the light around me will be night," even the darkness is not dark to You, and the night is as bright as the day. Darkness and light are alike to You.

PSALM 139:11–12 NASB

You have graduated, and you are probably in a hurry. Whatever your goals are, you don't want to let any grass grow under your feet. Standing a long time in a long line has no appeal. You want to hop a rapid transit and get there today.

Slow down. Take your time. Be patient. Study the pieces of the puzzle and see how each fits to make the big picture. Don't force them. Patience makes all things easier. Patience helps you stay when impatience makes you walk off. In the movie *Regarding Henry,* a rehabilitation counselor helps a brain-damaged man regain his power of speech because the counselor never loses his patience. He trusts that the long silences that precede Henry's first hesitant words are like periods of gestation where seeds are planted and begin to take root. He is willing and able to wait.

Patience waits on God to come and bring the help of his counsel, insight, and wisdom. It is never disappointed.

*H*e shall come down like
rain upon the grass before
mowing, like showers that
water the earth.

PSALM 72:6 NKJV

Where You Come From

*How very good and pleasant it is when kindred live
together in unity! It is like the precious oil on the head,
running down upon the beard, on the beard of Aaron.*

PSALM 133:1–2 NRSV

After graduation, you probably won't have the same physical proximity to your family. You will live in a different place, perhaps even far away. The sights, sounds, and smells you grew up with will no longer be there to call you to feeling, thought, and action. Mom, Dad, and siblings won't be your daily companions anymore. But don't forget your family. Remember where you come from.

A preschool teacher, wanting to remember the name of a new student, said, "Devin comes from heaven." The little guy responded, "No, I didn't. I came from my house." Remember in what ways you come from your house. Where you got your values and priorities, where your purpose was forged, your character developed. Where you learned how to regard other people. Where you learned the importance of God. Your family is the foundation on which you will stand and from which you will live your life.

*Wherever you go from here, you take your family with
you. Your family will be part of everything you do.*

LORD, you do
everything for me.
LORD, your love
continues forever.
Do not leave us,
whom you made.

PSALM 138:8 NCV

Use Freedom Well

Deal bountifully with Your servant, that I may live and keep Your word.
Open my eyes, that I may behold wonderful things from Your law.

PSALM 119:17–18 NASB

"Free at last," graduates sing as they throw their caps wildly in the air. Now you can do what you want to do. But is that true? A little boy asked his dad, "How long do I have to wait until I'm old enough to do what I want?" Dad replied, "That's a good question, and I can't say that I know the answer. Nobody's ever lived that long." Freedom is not what it's cracked up to be. It's much more.

Freedom is the privilege to become all God meant you to be. God intends more than for you to merely follow orders or to simply operate without restraint. God intends for you to carefully and prayerfully choose what you may and may not do according to how you understand God's will for your life. God wants you to use your freedom well.

Freedom is not being allowed to do as you please.
Freedom is being liberated to do what pleases God.

Praise the LORD, you his
angels, you mighty ones
who do his bidding, who
obey his word.

PSALM 103:20 NIV

Growing On

The righteous will flourish like a palm tree,
they will grow like a cedar of Lebanon.

PSALM 92:12 NIV

You're not through growing. Underneath the person you know yourself to be is the person God knows you to be. It is that person you can grow into. Dedicate your life to becoming who God has in mind. Be always creating fresh space for God to work in you and on you. A friend asked Henry Wadsworth Longfellow the secret of his continued zest for life. Pointing to a nearby apple tree, he said, "The purpose of that apple tree is to grow a little new wood each year. That is what I intend to do."

In the Talmud, a sacred text of Jewish law, traditions, and wisdom, there is a beautiful passage: *For every blade of grass, there is an angel bending over it, whispering, "Grow, grow."*

The largest room in your world is the room for improvement. Don't just go through life. Grow through life.

He brought me out into
a broad place; he
delivered me because
he delighted in me.

PSALM 18:19 NRSV

Good Habits Are Good

He leads humble people to do what is right, and he teaches
them his way. Every path of the LORD is one of mercy and truth
for those who cling to his promise and written instructions.

PSALM 25:9–10 GOD'S WORD

Some people always know what is right to do in any situation.
They don't have to think about it or consult anyone else. They just
do it, naturally. They just do it, from habit.
When you have good habits, you can respond
quickly to what needs to be done. Your habits
sit on your shoulder, instructing you what to
do. No deliberation is needed; no hesitation is
seen. Your progressive action comes from your
positive habits. Your good habits tell you what
God wants you to do.

A good habit is stronger than reason. You don't have to think out
a situation. A decision about it has been hammered out by consistent
repetition. You know it is the right thing to do because that's what it's
been for a long time. A good habit is better than inspiration.
Inspiration depends on too many variants. Habit depends on itself.

A good habit is a cable, woven together strand by strand
each day. When completed, it cannot be broken.

*G*od, be merciful to me because you are loving. Because you are always ready to be merciful, wipe out all my wrongs.

PSALM 51:1 NCV

A Helping Hand

*They will be so kind and merciful and good, that they will be a
light in the dark for others who do the right thing.*

PSALM 112:4 CEV

Among the goals you set for your future, be sure to put helping others high on your list. Graduation fills you with personal goals and dreams, but you'll need to remember to get beyond yourself to help others. Use your peripheral vision to see those who come from all sides. God sends them, and they need your help.

Helping others helps you. You don't put perfume on another without getting some of it splashed on yourself. Betty Ford said, "I don't think there's anything as wonderful in life as being able to help someone else." A real good exercise for the heart is to bend down and pick someone up who has fallen. Put that person on your shoulders and give him a lift. You will always stand taller with someone else on your shoulders. Help everyone you can. Be an equal opportunity servant.

*You accompany each act of service and are
present in each deed that helps others. When you
extend your hand, you extend yourself.*

The godly people in the land are my true heroes! I take pleasure in them!

PSALM 16:3 NLT

You Never Know

All who humble themselves before the Lord shall be given
every blessing, and shall have wonderful peace.

PSALM 37:11 TLB

One night, back in the 1960s, an African American woman stood on the side of an Alabama highway in a lashing rainstorm. Her car

had broken down. Soaking wet, she flagged the next car that came down the road. A young white man stopped and drove her to get a taxicab. She wrote down his address and sped away. Seven days went by, and a knock came on the young man's door. A large console television was delivered with a note attached: "Thank you for assisting me on the highway the other night. The rain drenched not only my clothes but my spirits. Then you came along. Because of you, I was able to make it to my dying husband's bedside before he passed away. God bless you for helping and unselfishly serving others." It was signed Mrs. Nat King Cole.

You never know who needs your help. Be ready and
willing to serve those whom God sends your way.

The LORD watches over
the lives of the innocent,
and their reward will
last forever.

PSALM 37:18 NCV

The Best Policy

Send out your light and your truth. Let them guide me. Let them bring me back to your holy mountain, to the place where you live.

PSALM 43:3 NIrV

As you go out to make a life for yourself, honesty in all things is an absolute necessity. Your integrity will be dictated by it, your character assessed by it. It will determine the quality of your friends and the depth of your friendships. It will decide the type of person you are perceived to be, and will lay bare your purest motives. It will escalate your success because people are needed who tell the truth. Honesty in all things will declare you close to the heart of God, and it will commend you as a person of spiritual dimension and influence.

A young man, who inquired over the phone if a business could use a hardworking, honest employee, learned they already had one. He hung up the phone, whistling. Asked by a bystander why he was happy, he replied, "Because I'm the hardworking, honest employee."

There is nothing so powerful as the truth. Know the truth, speak the truth, live what you know and speak.

Inspiring Words FROM THE PSALMS

*Y*ou desire truth in the inward being; therefore teach me wisdom in my secret heart.

PSALM 51:6 NRSV

Get Your Rest

I will both lie down in peace, and sleep; for You alone, O LORD, make me dwell in safety.

PSALM 4:8 NKJV

A long time ago, mattresses were secured on bed frames by ropes. When you pulled on the ropes, the mattress tightened, making the bed firmer to sleep on. That's where the phrase "Good night, sleep tight" came from. Whatever you do after graduation, your work during the day will require time, energy, and strength. Your mind and body will be tested during the day, and you will need to sleep tight at night.

While you sleep, God is at work. He is watching over you, holding you tightly in his arms of love. In that sense, the day doesn't begin in the morning but at night, when God tucks you in with prayer on his lips and passion in his heart. In the morning, you awake energized and ready to join God in the work the two of you will do that day.

A good night's rest rescues you from the day just past and refreshes you for the day to come.

I lie down and sleep, and all night long the LORD protects me. I am not afraid of the thousands of enemies who surround me on every side.

PSALM 3:5–6 GNT

Don't Be Afraid

*You, LORD, are the light that keeps me safe. I am not afraid
of anyone. You protect me, and I have no fears.*

PSALM 27:1 CEV

It's a great big world out there, but you don't have to be afraid.
The Bible uses the phrase "fear not" 365 times,
one for each day of the year. God wants you to
know he will help you with your fears. He does
not want them to hold you hostage or to dictate
who you are and determine what you do. God
doesn't want fear to victimize you. God doesn't
want fear of mistakes, missteps, or failures to
affect your confidence. Nor does God want fear
of commitment or fear of standing up for your
rights or fear of being alone to paralyze you.

When you stand in the shadow of fear, look beyond it to the
candles burning brightly in the window of God's knowledge and pro-
tection. God loves those he makes. God protects those he loves.

*The key to success is for you to make a habit
throughout your life of doing the things you
fear. God does them with you.*

In God, whose word I praise, in God I trust; I will not be afraid. What can mortal man do to me?

PSALM 56:4 NIV

Take Care of Business

He has given me a new song to sing, a hymn of praise to our God. Many will see what he has done and be astounded. They will put their trust in the LORD.

PSALM 40:3 NLT

A farmer along a seacoast had trouble getting workers because of the storms that raged there. A man applied for a job, and the farmer asked him if he was a good farm hand. The man replied, "I can sleep when the wind blows." The farmer didn't know what that meant but hired him anyway.

One night the wind howled, and the farmer jumped out of bed and rushed to the hired hand, who was sound asleep. He shook the man. "A storm is coming! Tie everything down!" The man rolled over and said, "No, sir. I told you, I can sleep when the wind blows." The angry farmer raced out to prepare for the storm. To his amazement, all the haystacks were covered, the cows were in the barns, the chickens were in the coops, and all the doors were barred. It was then he understood what the man meant.

An important key to success is self-confidence. An important key to self-confidence is preparation.

The LORD is my strength and my shield; my heart trusted in Him, and I am helped; therefore my heart greatly rejoices, and with my song I will praise Him.

PSALM 28:7 NKJV

Be a Leader

Hear my cry, O God; listen to my prayer. From the end of the earth I call to you, when my heart is faint. Lead me to the rock that is higher than I.

PSALM 61:1–2 NRSV

March up the aisle, out the door, and lead the way. Be a leader who stays close to the heart of God, loves the people of God, and takes them to the goals and plans of God.

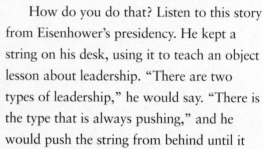

How do you do that? Listen to this story from Eisenhower's presidency. He kept a string on his desk, using it to teach an object lesson about leadership. "There are two types of leadership," he would say. "There is the type that is always pushing," and he would push the string from behind until it ended up in a wad. "Or there is the type that leads by pulling," and as he pulled the string along the desk, it would lengthen out and move forward. The best way to lead is to put your hand in the hand of God, get out in front, and pull people forward.

Faith, a commitment to something so strong that others find it contagious, is the most important qualification of a leader.

Oh, send out Your light and Your truth! Let them lead me; let them bring me to Your holy hill and to Your tabernacle.

PSALM 43:3 NKJV

Be a Follower

The LORD won't say no to his people. He will never desert those who belong to him. He will again judge people in keeping with what is right. All those who have honest hearts will follow the right way.

PSALM 94:14–15 NIrV

You won't always need to be a leader. Sometimes you will need to be a follower. A survey reported how many leaders came from only thirteen colonies but how few now come from fifty states. It suggested the problem is not a crisis of leadership but a crisis of *follower*ship. People are so independently minded that they refuse to follow.

At a fashionable college for women, the dean sent out a questionnaire to parents of incoming students. On the list was the question "Is your daughter a good leader?" Answers received, the dean wrote to one couple and said, "My dear friends, we're so glad you're sending your daughter to be a member of the first-year class. Inasmuch as the class is going to number 215 girls and we've already been assured of 214 good leaders, we are glad your daughter is coming along to be a follower."

Find those who lead to good and righteous places, and follow them. Above all else, follow God.

Happy are those who live pure lives, who follow the LORD's teachings. Happy are those who keep his rules, who try to obey him with their whole heart.

PSALM 119:1–2 NCV

Have a Good Life

Surely goodness and lovingkindness will follow me all the days of my life, and I will dwell in the house of the LORD forever.

PSALM 23:6 NASB

Perhaps the most damaging heresy in Christian history is the thought that Christian faith diminishes the wonder of life. Just the opposite, it invites you to acknowledge and celebrate in every way you can the good life God gives. Jesus said he came to give you life in all its fullness.

Life is not a journey to the grave with the intention of arriving in the best shape you can. Rather, life is a journey to the grave, skidding in sideways, comprehensively used up, entirely worn out, and loudly shouting, "Wow, what a ride!" God wants you to live in all the rooms of your life, not just in two or three of them. Remember that your lifework *is* your life. It is so true what Dr. Zhivago in Boris Pasternak's novel says: "We are born to live, not to prepare for life."

Claim your freedom and live; that's what life is about. Be good at life, and have a good life.

The LORD is my chosen portion and my
cup; you hold my lot. The boundary
lines have fallen for me in pleasant
places; I have a goodly heritage.

PSALM 16:5–6 NRSV

The Long Haul

God, my shepherd! I don't need a thing. You have bedded me down in lush meadows, you find me quiet pools to drink from. True to your word, you let me catch my breath and send me in the right direction.

PSALM 23:1–3 MSG

You have a long life ahead of you. Each morning your life begins, and it continues day after day. Days turn into years, years into decades, and decades into an average life span of 25,250 days. What will you do with all that time? Will you love life and let life love you back? Will you enjoy both the routine and the rapture? Will you be challenged by life when it is a mess, and give God glory when it is a masterpiece? Will you find your heart lifted in praise when life is a mix of mess and masterpiece?

Life is sometimes likened to a race. To have a good life, concentrate on the human race and not the rat race. Concentrate on how God, in a great variety of many ways, has generously and graciously blessed you.

Life is not a sprint. It is a distance event. Accompanied by the grace and mercy of God, go the distance.

*P*ray for the peace of Jerusalem: "May they
prosper who love you. Peace be within your
walls, prosperity within your palaces."

PSALM 122:6–7 NKJV

Take Some Risks

*Restore us, O LORD God Almighty; make your
face shine upon us, that we may be saved.*

PSALM 80:19 NIV

The greatest hazard in life is to risk nothing. If you risk nothing,
you do nothing and have nothing and—sometimes—are nothing. If

you take risks, you probably won't avoid
sorrow and suffering, but you will learn
what there is to learn and feel what there
is to feel. If you take risks, you will get
from where you are now to the place on
the map where God wants you to be. If
you take chances, you will grow from who
you are to the identity God has in mind
for you.

To launch a big ship, you need to go where the water is deep. Be
willing to go into the deep water. That's where success is. Remember
that Zacchaeus went out on a limb before he could see Jesus. Go out
on a limb; that's where the fruit is.

*When you risk going too far, you will find out how
far you can go. To get a return, take a risk.*

*Y*ou serve me a six-course
dinner right in front of my
enemies. You revive my
drooping head; my cup
brims with blessing.

PSALM 23:5 MSG

Two Sides of It

Words of wisdom come when good people speak for justice. They remember God's teachings, and they never take a wrong step.

PSALM 37:30–31 CEV

No matter how thin you slice it, there are two sides to everything. No matter how strongly you feel about something, God also gave the other person a mind with which to think and a heart with which to feel. Don't be so stiff in your opinion that you can't loosen up enough to consider the other side. Have a set of opinions, but be willing to rearrange them when you see wisdom come from another corner. Henry Ford said, "If there is any one secret to success, it lies in the ability to get the other person's point of view and see things from that angle as well as from your own."

There's a big world out there filled with intelligence and perception. Take the DO NOT DISTURB sign down from your assumptions, and open the door to the ideas and suggestions of others.

Wisdom comes from various places, insight from many sources. Wherever it comes from, receive it as God's gift to you.

*I*t is good for me to be near GOD; I have made the Lord GOD my refuge, to tell of all your works.

PSALM 73:28 NRSV

Opportunity Knocks

O God, you are my God, I seek you, my soul
thirsts for you; my flesh faints for you.

PSALM 63:1 NRSV

As a graduate, many opportunities are ahead of you. Keep your door open and stand on the threshold so you can see the possibilities and probabilities when they come up to your doorstep.

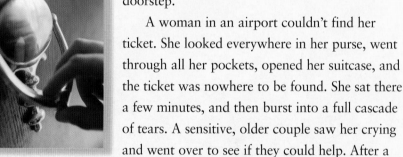

A woman in an airport couldn't find her ticket. She looked everywhere in her purse, went through all her pockets, opened her suitcase, and the ticket was nowhere to be found. She sat there a few minutes, and then burst into a full cascade of tears. A sensitive, older couple saw her crying and went over to see if they could help. After a while she calmed down, and the couple invited her to find a restaurant in the airport and eat lunch with them. She agreed, got up from her seat, and there was her ticket. She'd been sitting on it.

When the door is open, opportunity can come
in and make the smallest room large.
Opportunity has power everywhere.

The LORD looks down
from heaven and sees
every person.

PSALM 33:13 NCV

Look on the Bright Side

In God we have boasted continually, and we will
give thanks to your name forever.

PSALM 44:8 NRSV

Look on the bright side; it's good for your eyes. An optimistic outlook brings clarity of direction and clearness of destination. Through the eyes of optimism, you can see farther and you can see more. While others worry about the weeds, you see a garden filled with the beauty of God's flowers in every color and variety.

A man driving home from work stopped to watch a Little League baseball game being played in a park near his house. He sat down on the first-base line, and asked one of the young players what the score was. "We're behind fourteen to nothing," he answered with a surprising smile on his face. "Really?" the man said. "I have to say, you don't look very discouraged." "Discouraged?" the boy said with a puzzled look. "Why should we be discouraged? We haven't been up to bat yet."

Optimism is faith that leads to accomplishment and
achievement. Optimists make all things a possibility.

Let everyone bless God and sing his praises, for he holds our lives in his hands. And he holds our feet to the path.

PSALM 66:8–9 TLB

Solve Your Problems

The LORD pours down his blessings.
Our land will yield its bountiful crops.

PSALM 85:12 NLT

Three men had adjacent businesses in the same building. The businessman who ran the store at one end of the building put up a sign reading YEAR-END CLEARANCE SALE. At the far end of the building, the other businessman followed with a sign that said CLOSING-OUT SALE. The businessman in the middle knew what the other two had done would hurt his business, so he solved the problem by erecting a sign that said MAIN ENTRANCE.

You will have problems, and there will be ways to solve them. Problems are sometimes like a cowardly dog that growls and barks, but when you face that dog in firmness and with resolve, it backs away. A problem is something you can do something about. When you do something about a problem, it gets better.

A problem is the chance for you to call on God, do
your best, and believe an answer is on the way.

O Lord, you have been our
refuge throughout every
generation. Before the mountains
were born, before you gave birth
to the earth and the world, you
were God. You are God from
everlasting to everlasting.

PSALM 90:1–2 GOD'S WORD

Take Time to Play

*Let me go to the altar of God, to God of my highest joy, and I
will give thanks to you on the lyre, O God, my God.*

PSALM 43:4 GOD'S WORD

As a graduate, you are full of ambitions and goals. You want to
work hard and go far, but remember to play
along the way. All work and no play will make
you uninteresting to others and tedious to yourself. Recreation is exactly that, a re-creating of
your strength and power. At play, the interlude
of diversion and the refreshment of alternate
activity renew you, help restore your vision,
reclaim your goals, and reset your sights.

Play at its best lifts you out of where you
are and gives you a strong sense of where God is in your life. During
a children's sermon, a pastor was in the middle of a concluding
prayer when his four-year-old daughter climbed into his lap and blew
into his lapel mike. Distracted, he concluded his prayer by saying,
"In Christ's name we play."

*When play is sensible and wholesome, it gives
God a chance to break through your routine
and bless you with joy and delight.*

The LORD reigns, let the
earth be glad; let the
distant shores rejoice.

PSALM 97:1 NIV

Talk It Over with God

God has indeed heard me; he has listened to my prayer. I praise God, because he did not reject my prayer or keep back his constant love from me.

PSALM 66:19–20 GNT

As you go through the rest of your life, make prayer your partner. Talk everything over with God—your job, relationships, priorities, your goals. Put all activities and connections under the canopy of prayer. Itemize carefully, and leave nothing out. Converse with God about what you want in life and about what life does to you. Tell God how it feels to be you and how you'd like to feel about yourself as you turn the pages of the calendar and walk through the years. Discuss with God the people you know, and consult him about what they mean to you and what you want to mean to them.

Let God in on how you perceive yourself as a graduate facing the future. Delineate dreams and dares. Relate reservations and regrets. Tell it all to God.

There is nothing you can't talk to God about.
He will listen to everything.
He will hear everything.

God, hear my prayer.
Listen to what I'm saying.

PSALM 54:2 NIrV

Notes